To order
www. createspaces com/3718448

or
amazon . com

W9-CPJ-561

Christmas 2011

To Papa,

look on
page 21
for a poem
for a poem about you?

Angels

Unaware

by Vera deCicco

Enjoy the
quiet moments
that poetry
brings.
♡♡
love Vera

to order:
www. createspace. com/
3718448

Angels Unaware

Copyright © 2011 by Vera deCicco

Cover Art by Michelle Golias (www.michellegolias.com)
Bio Photo by Stephen Tocco

All rights reserved. No part of this book may be reproduced in any form by any electronic or mechanical means including photocopying, recording, or information storage and retrieval without permission in writing from the author.

ISBN-13: 978-0615564296
ISBN-10: 0615564291

Dunton Publishing
New York, New York
www.duntonpublishing.com

Dedication

This collection of poems is dedicated to the loving memory of my spiritual mentor Dr. Frederick J. Eikerenkoetter, who simply asked the question, "Are you publishing your poetry?" to which I can NOW answer, "Yes."

Acknowledgements

Special gratitude and appreciation to the three earth angels who encouraged, inspired and opened my heart to put the finishing touches in place.

Vera Marie, my daughter, for tirelessly transcribing the bits and pieces of hand written notes into print. Thank you for believing in me all these years, peace.

Michelle Golias, a gifted painter with a vision for beauty beyond what the eye can see. Thank you capturing the cover in light and love.

Lese Dunton, the most amazing ray of sunshine to come along and light the way. Thank you for igniting the flame and rekindling the spark of light to put this volume to print.

Forward

As I sit here, it appears that most if not all of my life has been a power struggle between me and my creator.

Me: Should I let you do it or do it myself??

Creator: Go within, listen, then act or not.

Me: That sounds too simplistic, I need to do something NOW. Don't you understand my life is falling apart, the world is falling apart. I need to do something NOW.

Creator: go within, listen, then act or not.

Me: Okay, how long, when and where? do I sit or kneel? Do I chant or breathe or affirm or visualize?

Creator: Go within, listen, then act or not.

Me: What is the "or not" about, do nothing?

Creator: go within, listen, act or not.

Me: Okay, I get it the "or not" is going deeper and listening.

Creator: Deeper and deeper.

Me: Can I do this deep listening on the subway, shopping or in the shower?

Creator: Go within, listen, then act or not.

Me: So I guess if I do this enough eventually it becomes constant, the trick is to listen in the midst of life.

Creator: I am with you always. Amen.

Description

This collection of poems is a tapestry of life as seen through the lens of a soul unfolding.

They came as messages softly whispering in my ear during moments of deep peace, intense stress, sometimes in the midst of teaming crowds or while walking alone along the path of light.

In any case these poems came through me as "angels unaware."

Table of Contents

Part 1

Table of Contents

Part 2

Part 2 - continued

Betweens

Between the tides
between the times
between the sheets
between friends
between the betweens
it seems as if
all things happen
between the betweens

Unbeknowns

Unbeknowns to the world
the heart grows
to fit the size
of fulfillment
she thought

So could it be that
the thing wished for
so passionately
cannot be recalled?

I must be doing it
she thought
sweetly
to herself

Vera deCicco

We Women

We Women
we cook
we sew
we bake
we wait

We Women
we quilt
we work
we birth
we love
we wait

We Women
we be
we pray
we stay
we women
we be

18

Intimacy

A rose arises
from the dust
of
vulnerability
opens
to
trust
emerges
in
pleasure
evolves
securely
in
care
and
knows
love

A Christmas Valentine

The heart
with
secrets
yet untold
will unfold
to know
itself
in secret
and
in
soul

Papa

Papa is
whistling
while
jingling
loose
change
in the
pocket
Papa is

Papa is
fixing
some
stuffed
peppers
or
greens and
beans
Papa is

Papa is
wisecracking
laughing
at life
sharing joy
cutting hair
taxiing
bicycling
swimming
Papa is

Papa is
praying
staying
sweet
whistling
while
jingling
loose
change
in the pocket
Papa is

Mother of Pearl

In a quiet moment
she took the time
to re-string her
Mother's pearls

A double strand
rather long and flowing
the clasp still held
securely on her
Mother's pearls

She ought to wear them
more often now
her Mother's pearls

I Love You

I love you
I thankyou
I love you
I believe you
I love you
I accept you
I love you
and so it goes

One

Everything is ONE
the wind is ONE
the mind is ONE
I AM ONE
I AM THE ONE
I AM THAT ONE

Amen

The Poet

the poet
on the phone
the poet
part of me
likes to be
alone
and yet
I like
people too
on the phone!

A Way of Being

Time has a way of
being timeless
Space has a way of
being spaceless
Love has a way of
being endless
Body has a way of
being bodiless
Feeling has a way of
being emotionless
Thought has a way of
being thoughtless
Self has a way of
being selfless
Being has a way
of being.

Now and Then

Now and Then
mostly then
to save the
NOW

Sometimes forward
into when

NOW is riper
than
then or when

She is NOW
NOT
then or when

Buttons

The leather button
popped off
the green sports coat
she inherited from
her Dad

The thing just rotted off
the rest of it looked good
right color good fit nice flare

So what's a button
here or there?

No one will miss it
but me

Italian Girls

Italian girls - what is it about them
that makes them so sexy and so raw?

It must be all those can'ts and don't dos
Growing up with so many rules

Italian girls - like naked cheeks in the
sun
love fun

Italina Girls

What is it that makes a Man a Man to a Woman?

What is it that makes
a man a man
to a woman?

Is it money?
It is sex?
It is shelter?
Is it protectiveness?
Is it tenderness?
Is it closeness?
Is it roughness?
Is it coldness?
Is it caring?
Is it thrills?
Is it romance?
Is it taking out the garbage?

Just what is it that makes
a man a man
to a woman?

Is it companioning?
Is it cooking?
Is it cuddling?
Is it nesting?
Is it roaming?

Is it dependability?
Is it handsomness?
Is it ruggedness?
Is it gentlemanliness?
Is it directness?
Is it masterfulness?
Is it sweetness?

Just what is it that makes
a man a man
to a woman

Is it wisdom?
Is it faithfulness?
Is it strength?
Is it love?
Is it power?
Is it imagination?
Is it willingness?
Is it understanding?
Is it correctness?
Is it enthusiasm?
Is it discernment?
Is it aliveness?

It is all of the above
in love!

No Comfort

No comfort in
this couch

No comfort
in food

No comfort
in the phone

No comfort
in friends

No comfort
in films

No comfort
in books

No comfort
in music

No comfort
in sex

*No comfort
in family*

*No comfort
in money*

*No comfort
in the floor*

*No comfort
in clothes*

*No comfort
inside*

*No comfort
in comfort*

*No comfort
in prayer*

*No comfort
in work*

*No comfort
in taking*

*No comfort
in talking*

*No comfort
in words*

*No comfort
in houses*

*No comfort
in cars*

*No comfort
in pills*

*No comfort
in shoes*

*No comfort
in candles*

*No comfort
in smiles*

*No comfort
in hugs*

No comfort
in kisses

No comfort
in kids

No comfort
in fights

No comfort
in planes

No comfort
in trains

No comfort
in beds

No comfort
in chairs

No comfort
in baths

No comfort
in dreams

No comfort
in comfort

No comfort
in candy

(an unfinished poem)

or so she thought
the comfort
comes in
the openness
of knowing
no comfort

A Simple Soup

What it all boils down to
is a simple soup
bits and pieces
odds and ends
leftovers
and uncooked
dried peas

This place needs a simple soup
some yellow split peas
some sun dried tomatoes
some macaroni shells
some spices from
a mail-ordered Christmas present
and lots of love

As I keep the word in my heart hidden
so I might not rock the boat too much

A simple soup
to soothe the rough places
in life
it simmers and stews
the color quickens
and thickens to a

rich creamy
yellowish, reddish
pink
a simple soup
and thee

Frozen Roses

Have you ever
walked by
a garden in
early November
when all the roses
were
freshly in bloom
and the first frost
freezes
them in the midst
of beauty
brittle and fragile
like styrofoam
stilled in the moment
spectacular!

Flies Don't Die

Flies don't die
neither do I
They simply rearrange
themselves
back into themselves
appearing to disappear

Flies don't die
neither do I

Spring is

Spring is
the softness
of moss
the gentleness
of fern
the velvet
of a caterpillar's coat
the flutter
of a robin's wing
in mid-air
the bee gathering
sweet nectar
from here to there
the crocus sprouting
out thru snowy spots

Spring is
the season of
things hoped for
but not yet seen
the time of seeds
the promise of
fulfillment
the budding of the Rose

Vera deCicco

the freshness of the
breeze
the veil is pierced
and new life
emerges
Spring is

Late Winter / Early Spring

the beauty of the
blossoms
in early spring

delicate and flowing
upon
the remnants
of the late winter's
last snow

evidence
of resolution
where two
seasons
intertwine

late winter
early spring

August rain

as the moon
approaches
fullness
so do I
sleeping face
toward shining
moon
not quite full
clear and clean
after August's
rain
so am I

Silver Rain

Silver rain teaming
in sheets
across the open
window
what made it shine?
the sun's glistening
silver streaks

Silver rain
shining
gleaming
like needles
of light
piercing
the
earth

Snow Thunder

A soft rumbling
heard thru
the snow's silence
like a roaring
whisper
snow thunder

a quiet reminder
that two
elements can
intertwine
and be
distinctly different
Snow thunder

Late Bloomer

a rose
buds in
Spring

a rose
blooms in
Summer

a rose
blossoming
in Fall
tells it all

the blush of an
autumn
Rose
is
a mixture of
sweet sadness

Summer passes
Sun remains
to bring forth
beauty
Late Bloomer

Snow Blossoms

Snow Blossoms
timeless truth
when friendship
turns to love
and love turns
into friendship
turning
turning
over and over
'til both
become
as
ONE

Winter's Coat

Winter's coat
she threw it off
the winter's coat
like a
lizard sheds
old skin
it lay all
crumpled in the chair
with torn pockets
and worn sleeves
stained and strained
at the seams
frayed
forlorn
winter's coat

Summer Citying

skateboarding
basketballing
rollerblading
ice creaming
sunsetting
dream blossoming
Summer citying

T-shirting
class listening
video viewing
flower watching
butter flying
mango munching
Summer citying

bus hopping
train catching
conference taping
carrot crunching
Summer citying

meditating
blender buzzing

prayer blessing
clothes washing
feet baring
Summer citying

letter writing
quilt sewing
hair cutting
Summer citying

floor mopping
love hugging
children kissing
legs tanning
Summer citying

breath breathing
heart opening
ear phoning
I AM-ing
Summer citying

self revealing
city summering
Summer simmering
herbal teaing

mid-night peeing
sweet city
summering

silk dressing
sandal slipping
peace prevailing
city summering

Steam Heat

Wonder if the heat's
about to start up

So far it's kind of cold
and still no steam

Not even a rattle
a hiss or a bang
like when the world
began

Just stillness

Wonder when the
heat's coming up?

Socks

The change of weather
prompts some socks

Still I like to hold on to Summer
a bit longer
by going sockless

Something daring and
reckless about being
sockless in October

Wouldn't you?

Part 2

Of Eagles and Angels

Of Eagles and Angels

the soul knows
how to soar
above life's
human woes
and rejoice
in sweet
refrains
of how it grows
of eagles and angels
being above the scene
touching the earth
so serene
eagles and angels
tell of wonders beyond
to gently show the way
amen.....

Cactus flower

for every
prickly
thorny
chapter in
life
a blessing
blossoms......

The Last Lazy Days

the last lazy
days of summer
are fading into fall
still a bit
of flowers remain
thru it all
gold yellow
orange red
summer's stillness
rides the air
peaking before
they disappear.......

Grandmothered

how to know
a grandmother
when you see her
her socks
don't match
her hair is
a mess
her smile
is glowing
her feet are swift
when she plays
all day in the backyard
grandmothered
when she
cancels dates
to babysit
wears froggie
pajamas
eats peanut butter
plays the ukulele
fingerpaints
rolls on the floor
makes the

stuffed animals
talk and
loves to cuddle
grandmothhered.........

A Portable Life

it seems as if
our lives
can fit into
a megabyte
so concentrated
and compact
no need for a
large backpack
in the cosmic
scheme of things
we can all
but disappear
into techno air
and be contained
within a small frame
of a tiny screen
bearly seen
is that really you
of just a
flashing light
in view
the smallest dot
and all that
we possess

is portable
transferable

collaspable
and impermanent
as an
ant
scurrying across
the earth........

Vera deCicco

Am I MY Eyebrows

am I my eyebrows
fading
fading
slowly fading
out of sight
and yet
a faint outline
of white hairs remain
where once
the brow began
am I my eyebrows
or am I
fading
fading
fading
out of sight
with only
a glimmer
of white light
where once
my body stood
to be continued
on the
lighter side
of life.......

64

Reflections of a Butterfly

if you stay
the same
and
I change
what happens
notthing or
everything
you either notice
the change or
not
if you notice
the change
did I change
or did you
neither and
both
in remaining
unchanged
are you
unaffected
by my change
yes and no
so I change
again

and you remain
the same

or do you
it's all the
the point of view
by observing
your change
am I changed
yes and no
we both change
and remain
changeless
in the
exchange.....

The Love Seat

two cushions
pressed into a
rounded frame
with soft arms
and an embracing back
the love seat
the first sign
of comfort in their
little lovenest
over the years
company came
walls were removed
boundaries extended around
the love seat
the color changed
objects were lodged
beneath the surface of
the love seat
it became a haven
a refuge
an island of delight
for visitors
family and friends
alike

the love seat
one special visitor
from a small planet
especially enjoyed
nesting on
the love seat
sometimes the pillows
were dislodged and served
as a landing pad
for resting relatives
or overnight guests
on the floor
the love seat
adjustable
adaptable
accommodating
the love seat
love is like that......

Two Silver Birds

I saw in the sky today
high above the
Central Park
landscape
two silver birds
flying very high
in perfect
synchronicity
each with the
exact sameness
in flight
as they dipped
and glided
and swerved
and dived and rose
together
in perfect harmony
in one graceful
swoop
and disappeared
into the sun......

This and That

there is this and that
"this" can be a stack of
books piled high
upon the bed
and "that" can be
and empty wooden
fruit waiting to be filled
"this" can be a pile of
opened mail
unsorted and unread
"that" can be bunches of
business cards
collected for future
reference
"this" can be notepads
all sizes
small medium and large
with pages all askew
"that" can be the silenced
answering machine
green light aglowing
"this" can be a breakfast
made from odds and ends

tofu apple and grains
"that" can be a clean
set of sheets to
freshen up the day
"that" can be a bill
from the IRS for
unpaid taxes
"this" can be a snap of
neck that releases
unexpressed energy
"that" can be a smile
a hug
a handshake
we are ONE.......

Horseshoe Crabs Mating

the horseshoe crabs are
mating by the shore
working in a pattern
a rhythm
I never saw before
they get real
close and then
stick to one
another's shell
rocking
in the waves
'til the bubbles
foam and flee
what a thing to see
horseshoe crabs
mating
excuse me........

By the Window

the handy man's helper
chopped
the hedges too low
outside the window
so now the world seems
too close
by the window
stark and naked
right there
so to speak
by the window
passersby get clearer
and so do I
by the window......

Vera deCicco

Wash and Wear

wash and wear
not jus a slogan
but a life style
the dry cleaning method
did not appeal to
her aesthetic sense
of wholeness
the chemicals
did not feel clean
so close to the skin
or was it the silent
toxins of synthetics
wash and wear
all natural fibers
have always felt
closer to
natural life
the allness
of all cotton
the pureness
of pure silk
the softness
pure wool

wash and wear
the rain fell on
the lamb
the sun shone on
silk wormned the earth and wind
nurtured the cotton seed

so why use dry cleaners
I suppose to iron
out wrinkles
she goes with the wrinkles
for twenty years now
without ironing.......

Soul Searching

am I obsessing
am I overdosing
on neo oriental philosophy
am I overlooking
words of truth
am I too passive
am I too aggressive
is it all pleasure
is it all pain
or all feasting
or all fasting
is transcendence
suppression in disguise
do will and ego
go hand and hand
to serve the delights or delusions
does prayer and meditation
coincide or collide
or are they just
manipulations of the mind
the monkey mind that
fluctuates without a master
alas alas

the rain is stilling
sustaining
soothing
and one does not question
the rain
it simply is
an element of love
beware the head
the heart is seeking
self awareness
self realization
self fulfillment
self love
self alignment
unification
the flower sees
the gentle breeze
the earth renews
thru water
a tree clutching
to it's dry and lifeless branches
ceases to grow
the storm rips
apart the weakest limbs
renewal takes place
new growth begins

new strength surges up
amid the core
and so it is with love
just looking out the window
the self is seen
in rapid similarity
turning in
the petals cease to flutter
quite so frantically
the heart surrounds
the mind seductively
and I am one with thee
and thee with me........

In The Midst of an Eclipse

let's begin all over again
here in the midst of an eclipse
muddled befuddled
miffed tiffed
we scramble and ramble
so what else is new
priests and physicians
ministers and magicians
what about rabbis and gurus
nothing new under the sun
we all get to see beneath
the covers from time to time
and peek at eternity
in a glance
amen.

Supermarket Opening Day

supermarket opening day
the sidewalk
buzzed with
plastic shopping bags
stuffed along
the way
supermarket opening day
flags flapping furiously
delicacies left and right
she breezed in
that's right
it was ash wednesday
to boot
so all the little ladies
in the neighborhood
had dots on
their foreheads
giving the third eye
a holiday
peeking out
to see
on
supermarket opening day

the message
when you stop
to see
the dust of ages past
the dust of days to come
could not defer
supermarket opening day
ho hum...........

Dream Reflections

I am you
the walk
the manner of speech
the curl in the hair
I am you
the soonest thought
the closest touch
the torn tear
I am you
pulled thread
forgotten song
dark night
I am you
in all
the glory
and pain
YOU.......

Lord of Love

the day is framed
by the light of
learning
learning one's self
thru
reading
listening
seeing
others
face to face
placing the heart
in the hand
ever so
gently......

Pockets

pockets keep the
precious threads
of life
contained
keys
lipstick
gloves
glasses
letters to mail
mailed letters
pens
loose change
hankies
notes and lists
indeed
pockets on the outside
of a coat
pockets
on the inside
of a skirt
shirt pockets
pants pockets
pockets in the
checkbook
in the notebook
pockets in your

boots
pockets in the
mind
mind pockets
what size
what shape
is the mind pocket
of kindness
of gentleness
of remembrance
some mind pockets
are empty of gladness
others bulging with love
there is the love pocket
the petty pocket
the pocket of anger
the pocket of hesitation
the pockets of
patience
peace
persistance
yes the mind has
many pockets
and as we see
the heart is
a pocket
pockets of the heart
are cups of compassion

Vera deCicco

wells of wholeness
the ears are pockets
of grace
and so it goes
pocket to pocket......

The Hair Cut

she wandered
her way
along
Washington square park
thru the NYU campus
to Astor Place
watching winter wane
and spring spring
the barber's pole
flashed red white and blue
in she stepped
to her new look
cut off the old dead
ends of winters' weary song
keep it short and sweet
for spring
refreshed and new again
the barber's chair
stood at attention
the barber had prepared
his swiftly tuned
scissors
chop chop
sculpting and sweeping

to the disco beat
the new look
emerged
like a crocus or
tulip
she popped up
happy to be home
again
the barber shop
was home you see
she grew up in one
her papa being one
a barber
from the old country
the other side
the atmosphere
was so familiar
no frills
no more fancy uptown
hair salons
that snipe it here
and snipe it there
and charge a king's ransome
just give her the barber shop
home again.......

The Hockey Game

it was an away
game
bi-partisan
group
not the
usual crowd
he said
they ate
ham and egg salad
sandwiches
in the car
changed clothes
put on this
sweat shirt
he said
once inside
the atmosphere
was likened
to a huge
space ship
complete with
popcorn
the ice
beamed white

once seated
he told her
the rules of the game
amid cheers and boos
smiles and
concerned stares
the game glided on
he tried to hide
his disappointment
behind a grim glare
keep you words
sweet
you may have to
eat them
along with
that hat
she told him
they laughed
the score was
six to three
the rain
outside
the
stadium was
torrential
the waves

*of affection
and understanding
stood above
it all
as mother
and son
moved
along
the highway......*

Enlightenment

sun beaming
gleaming
across 125th street
on the IRT
number one local
broadway line
surfacing above ground
just a
glimpse
of rooftops
a ray of light
toward
a new day
pushing
shoving
along the way
stillness in the sun
enlightenment..........

Tapestry

The I LOVE NEW YORK
canvas shopping bag
has been serving
as a tote bag since
the holidays
it transports
lunch
the Times
fruit
books
bills
and various other sundries
thru slush sleet ad snow
along the rough edges of the
IRT number one local
it is collapsible and sustaining
it is enduring and endearing
the message is clear
I LOVE NEW YORK........

Nearness

the breath of a
baby
nearness
the touch of a
feather
nearness
the comfort of a
friend
nearness
the peace of a
prayer
nearness
the sound of
no sound
nearness
the light in
the darkness
nearness
amen.

Winter

It's winter inside
my room
of seasons
how did it get here
so fast
I guess I wasn't
paying attention
to the subtle signs
as they inched in
first the frost
then the wind
lots of rain
to fall the leaves
and finally snow
and ice to replace
sun's warmth
amen.

Above All Things

above all things
there is a riff
a conflict
a wrestling
of sorts
opposing
currents
of thought
battling it out
underneath the surface
just below
the level of being
and yet it all ties into lies
upon lies of what lies ahead
amen.

Geraniums

my geraniums are happy
my soul sings
and dances
in sheer delight
for the joy
of being
vitally
alive
and
the geraniums
are happy......

Fish

we are like fish
in a big fish bowl
swimming around and around
floating passed one another
like fish in a big fish bowl
light and weightless
free and yet aware of our
boundaries
respect abides
as the path unfold
like fish swimming around
in a big fish bowl
looking for water......

Pages

there are pages
without numbers
there are places
without faces
there are spots
in the earth
that are filled
with much worth
there are rivers
with no names
there are children
with no games
there are pages
with no numbers
there are poems
waiting to be penned
there are unheard
songs from a friend
amen.

The Cause

'cause it is too easy
'cause it is too hard
'cause I am a woman
'cause I am single
'cause I am over fifty
everyone's got a cause
'cause it s too late
'cause it is too early
'cause it is too expansive
'cause it is too cheap
'cause it is too healthy
'cause it is too natural
'cause it is too convenient
'cause it is too available
everyone's got a cause
'cause it is too cold
'cause it is too hot
'cause it is mine
'cause it is yours
'cause it is right
'cause it is wrong
everyone's got a cause
'cause it is on TV

'cause it is in church
'cause it is in the news
'cause it is in Paris
'cause it is in NYC
'cause it is in India
'cause it is in New Jersey
'cause it is in Brooklyn
everyone's got a cause
there is only
one cause
the first cause
the light
of everyone's
being
amen.

Step by Step

step by step
turn by turn
we learn
in the turning
we return
from doubting
to knowing
we turn
from fear
to confidence
we turn
from outer
to inner
we learn
we turn
step by step
we grow
we know......

Circles

circles bend
and flex
and contain
a trick
or two
in the turning
be like a circle
continuously touching
never apart
returning
into itself
a circle
that opens up
to itself
from within
itself
be like that
to one another

Letting GO

fading
letting go
of heaviness
letting go
of the grip
letting go
of the drama
letting go of
the game
letting go of
letting go.....

Can You Canoe

can you canoe
can we give each other
a clue as to how to
canoe
it is simple to
canoe
just put in your
paddle and canoe
you can do it
canoe canoe
get it
you too can canoe
with that simple clue
paddle paddle
canoe canoe
can you......

Beyond Stillness

there is
deep deep
stillness
so deep
that it
can only
be felt
in the
void
of
no breath
deeper still
in non being
the still of
stillness
beyond stillness
the light
beyond light
the being
beyond being
the beginning
beyond all
beginnings.......

Gentle Rain

the softness
of the
gentle rain
misting thru
the morn
asking only
to be born
the earth weeps
and smiles
and throws off
loud roars of
laughter
at man's folly....

Under The Trees

under the trees
in the meadow
with jets
zooming overhead
near the river
sat a group of ten
gathered in a circle
to thank
the mother earth
the rain gently
caressed us all
as we prayed
sang
and touched
the earth
to say
THANK YOU
we smiled
hugged
and moved on.....

And It Came To Pass

the chaos
the confusion
the pain, anger, hurt
the denial, surrender
the calm, peace
love and compassion
and it came to pass
the birds barely chirping
shaken crumbled and collapsed
and it came to pass
silent skies
saddened eyes
and it came to pass
sirens screaming
tears streaming
and it came to pass
touching sharing
thoughts comparing
candles burning
hearts yearning
peace returning
and it came to pass.....

Polyester Dresses and Plastic Shoes

polyester dresses
and plastic shoes
in a world of
natural organic
origins
how is it we
manage to make
polyester dresses
and plastic shoes
so sleek and slippery
looks so real
feels so soft
but wait a minute
the stuff sticks
clings and sweats
no open pores in
polyester dresses
and plastic shoes
they never wear out
wash in the machine
and pack without wrinkles
yet somehow
the skin knows

the difference
between
polyester dresses
and plastic shoes
the lightness
of silk
the warmth
of wool
the sweetness
of cotton
nature embracing
the skin
and so it goes
the polyester dresses
and plastic shoes
are not biodegradable
and will continue on
into eternity
while we
linger in the NOW
wondering
HOW did these
polyester dresses
and plastic shoes
get here

10301674R00071

Made in the USA
Charleston, SC
24 November 2011